Would You
RATHER?
QUESTIONS
FOR
COUPLES

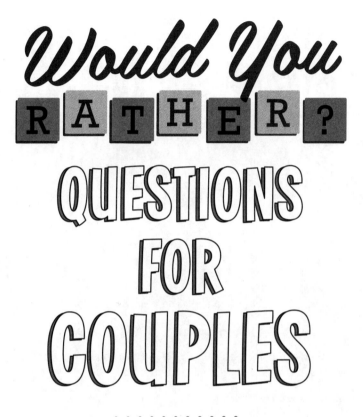

Would You RATHER?

QUESTIONS FOR COUPLES

Laugh and
Grow Closer with
Fun Conversations

SANJI & TAYLOR MOORE

ZEITGEIST · NEW YORK

Published in the United States by Zeitgeist, an imprint of Zeitgeist™, a division of Penguin Random House LLC, New York.

penguinrandomhouse.com

Zeitgeist™ is a trademark of Penguin Random House LLC

ISBN: 9780593436103
Ebook ISBN: 9780593436097

Cover illustration © Anastasiia Ivanova/Shutterstock.com
Cover design by Aimee Fleck
Interior design by Erin Yeung
Edited by Ada Fung

Printed in the United States of America

3rd Printing

First Edition

To Dan, Eric, Mark, Laura, and Dana.
Thanks for the introduction.

Contents

Introduction

Welcome, reader, to the wild, wild world of Would You Rather! There's a decent chance you've played some version of this game before, but if you haven't, don't worry. It's simply a way to learn about yourself and your partner while having a few laughs. Or, in our case, Would You Rather helped us fall in love.

About a decade ago, we were out on a date together—maybe our fourth or fifth? (Point is, it was enough times to know whether we really liked the other person and short enough to ghost them for admitting their love of cold cuts.) The conversation was dying, so in a moment of awkward panic, Sanji asked Taylor, "Uhhhh, which sandwich would you rather eat: turkey with sliced pepper jack cheese, tomato, pickled onion, and mayo on ciabatta bread or shrimp with avocado, vinegar-based coleslaw, and grilled zucchini in a wrap?" Silence ensued—was it too weird to deal with or too fun to turn away from?

Finally: "Is the shrimp grilled or fried?" Taylor asked.

A few years later, we were married.

You might be thinking, *Can a question about sandwiches really have brought you two together?*

Well, it's not just about the question; it's about how you engage with it. What follow-up questions does your partner ask? Why did they choose one option over the other? You might just be surprised how much you can learn about your partner's history, interests, priorities, and what makes them tick—all by playing this game.

Or, they could choose not to play at all—in which case, you'll know they're zero fun and that you should absolutely dump them.

We wrote this book to create a fun way for couples to spend time together, understand each other, surprise each other, and be a little silly. In it, you'll find more than 250 Would You Rather questions organized into seven themes. The question topics range from the mundane and everyday to the impossible and bizarre, with scenarios involving celebrities, superpowers, or other absolute nonsense. We've even included questions on big philosophical problems and those whose answers could decide the fate of the entire human species—so, choose wisely! There's something here for everyone.

Now, go ahead and give it a try.

We'll start you off: Would you rather turn the page and have a fun night or put down this book and stare at the wall?

How to Use This Book

There's no right or wrong way to use this book. Feel like flipping to a random page? You're going to have a good time. Or are you more the type to work through every question in order? You do you! In this section, we offer ideas for using the questions. For example, they can simply be a launching pad for conversations that make you laugh. Or they can serve as the basis for a no-holds-barred competitive game with rules and points. The most important thing (as always) is that you have a good time.

We've played Would You Rather a million times— in brief moments between errands, at a beach house when a hurricane knocked the power out, and across the dinner table when neither of us wanted to go to bed. We hope you enjoy it as much as we have . . . and still do.

MAKE TIME FOR FUN AND GAMES

We all lead busy lives, so it can be tough to find space for quality time together. Would You Rather questions are lightweight and easy to slide into whatever part of your day needs a bit more fun. Maybe you're in a new relationship, or maybe you've been together so long you've already talked about everything else. Either way, anytime the conversation starts to flag, you've got an ace in your back pocket with these questions. Just say, "Hey, a friend of mine asked me this [great/hilarious/ really hard] question the other day." And then let loose. Pick the right question, and you've just bought yourself another hour of good conversation. Plus, you'll know your partner better afterward.

Play Text-a-Question. You don't have to be face-to-face to spice up each other's day with Would You Rather. If you're like us, with both partners working long hours, it can be tough to find time for fun or to talk about anything not related to work or housekeeping. So, the next time you're missing your partner during the workday, text them a Would You Rather question. They can respond immediately or take the day to properly ponder the question and give their final answer when you see each other again. It's a gift to end the day with something fun.

Pass your partner secret notes. We love this one. Write a question on a slip of paper and hide it somewhere your partner will find it. We've found secret notes in holes in the brick wall near our bed, taped to the inside of yogurt lids, and buried in our dog's kibble. It's a hilarious surprise. Every. Single. Time.

Hold a game night. Add some pens and paper to make it feel more structured and . . . voilà! You've got a fun low-stakes game night for two. Each partner writes down five questions on slips of paper from any section in this book and then each takes a turn picking one from a bowl (or a hat or an old turtle shell you found in the desert). Feeling more competitive? In the next section, we'll go over ways to turn the questions into a game.

VARIATIONS ON THE GAME

Now, you don't have to turn these questions into a game. They can be free-form investigations into your hidden preferences and unexplored desires, sprung at a moment's notice. But maybe the dangerous flame of competition flickers deep inside both of you. In that case, use the following ideas for gamifying the Would You Rather questions that appear in this book.

The Psychic. You'll be familiar with this one if you've seen *The Newlywed Game*. The psychic knows and sees all: the way to win is by correctly predicting which option your partner or other players—you can play this with any number of people—will choose. Take turns selecting a question and reading it aloud. Immediately write down what you think the other or others will choose. Then reveal your answer to see if you guessed correctly. Or, if you want to incorporate more conversation, discuss the question for five minutes before writing down your guess. Do this seven times, and whoever gets the most correct guesses wins. If you tie, you must get married or renew your vows within five business days. (Just kidding . . . Or are we?)

The Rather Master. It's the Rather Master's world; we're just living in it. It can be played by any number of people, but it works for only two as well. First, choose the Rather Master. This person will pick a question, but before they read it aloud to the others, they will consider the options and decide which is the "correct" answer. (Yes, it's ridiculous, but also fun.) The other person (or persons) can ask the Rather Master questions to try to suss out the "correct" answer. For instance, if the question is "Would you rather have to wear a suit of fried chicken skin or eat a suit of fried chicken skin every day?" you could ask the Rather Master, "Does the chicken skin taste good?" or "In this world, are other people also wearing chicken-skin suits?" Once the players have made their choice, the Rather Master reveals the "correct" answer. Repeat this five times.

ABC, or Always Be Choosing. This one's for the extroverts and salespeople in the crowd. It's best played with at least three people—finally, something for throuples! (Or, you know, group game night.) Choose a question at random. One person will be the advocate for option A and another person will be the advocate for option B. The advocates then make their best sales pitch to the rest of the group. Questions are welcome, but not from the other advocate—it's a sales floor, not a courtroom. Each advocate gets one point for every person who votes for their option. Do this until there's a clear winner or until everyone has to go home anyway. Make it extra spicy by having two couples compete against each other. Or, if it's just the two of you playing, you can both vote on who you think gives the better argument—if you agree to play fair!

WINNER, WINNER, CHICKEN DINNER

It's right there in the name: the loser must cook a chicken dinner for the winner. Pro tip: To get the chicken skin extra crispy, make sure it's as dry as possible before you put it in the oven. We've even used a hair dryer. Sounds crazy, but it works like magic.

If you don't eat chicken, or if this just isn't your idea of a good time, here are some other suggestions for prizes:

- ❤ ▦ The loser must re-create the winner's favorite child-hood meal at home. The winner has to say it's good.

- ❤ ▦ The loser must treat the winner to a "spa day" at home. This is a fancy name for lighting a candle and giving them a back rub, but it's still nice, no matter what you call it.

- ❤ ▦ The loser must give the winner a surprise treat. This can be a fun-size candy bar or some other small item, hidden in a place where the winner is sure to find it. The funnier the place, the better.

- ❤ ▦ The winner gets to pick the temperature of your shared space for a set time. Be careful. Absolute power *can* corrupt absolutely.

- ❤ ▦ The winner gets to choose the lock and background image on the loser's smartphone. Have fun, but be nice!

- ❤ ▦ The loser must draw a portrait of the winner, taking their time and making it as true to life as they can. The loser must then frame and hang the portrait.

QUESTIONABLE LIFE CHOICES

Decisions are hard, especially when it comes to the essentials of life. In this chapter, you'll make tough choices about food, fashion, style, career, hygiene, and pretty much anything else you care about. Most of these are permanently life-altering decisions, so choose wisely!

Would you rather
have to survive being lost on
a mountain range
or
in a rainforest with your partner?

Would you rather
have to dress fancy
or
in sweats, no matter the situation,
for the rest of your life?

Would you rather
always be 20 minutes late
or
20 dollars short whenever you're
out with your partner?

Would you rather
that everything you ate for the rest
of your life tasted like pizza
or
that you were never able to
taste pizza again?

Would you rather
have all food taste delicious to you
or
have all songs sound like
total bangers?

Would you rather
have a permanent splinter in your toe
or
a permanent paper cut
on your finger?

Would you rather
sing operatically whenever
you spoke
or
square-dance whenever you
walked with your partner?

Would you rather
have toes for fingers
or
fingers for toes for the
rest of your life?

Would you rather
be forced to eat sandwiches
that are sopping wet
or
sandpaper-dry?

Would you rather
never be able to eat cake again
or
never drink wine again?

Would you rather
always win at everything
but never have fun
or
always be a loser but
always have fun?

Would you rather
be able to wear only clothes
that are a size too big
or
a size too small?

Would you rather
be forced to share a bathroom
or
a closet for the rest of your life?

Would you rather
give up brushing your teeth forever
or
have a partner who never
brushes theirs?

Would you rather
give up access to the internet
or
the ability to have orgasms
for the rest of your life?

Would you rather
travel with your partner
only by skateboard
or
only by tandem bike?

Would you rather
walk only in flippers
or
only in wooden clogs for
the rest of your life?

Would you rather
be able to only shout
or
only whisper?

Would you rather
have to only walk backward
or
only speak backward (no
explanations allowed with either)?

Would you rather
give up good wine
or
good cheese forever?

Would you rather
only be able to wake up at 3 a.m.
or
3 p.m. for the rest of your life?

Would you rather
be able to go to space one time
but never travel again
or
travel wherever you wanted for
the rest of your life but never
go to space?

Would you rather
have to eat your food blended
up and through a straw
or
eat food so crunchy it cuts up the
roof of your mouth all the time?

Would you rather
go on a 15-hour road trip with your
partner in a car with broken speakers
or
with broken heating and AC?

Would you rather
never be able to eat a burger
or
chocolate again?

Would you rather
be free of debt
or
free of guilt?

Would you rather
work more hours and have
longer weekends
or
only work half days but not
have weekends off?

Would you rather
always be crippled by self-doubt
even when you know what you're
talking about
or
plagued by overconfidence even
when you're totally wrong?

Would you rather
lose all the memories you've
made in the last five years
or
all the money you've earned
in that period?

Would you rather
never have a pet for the rest
of your life
or
have so many that your house
smelled bad but you didn't know it?

Would you rather

spend your life deeply bonded to
a super-smart gorilla sidekick,
but no one thinks that's cool,

or

be able to talk to animals
you have zero connection to,
but everyone thinks you're
cool for being able to do it?

Would you rather

wake up every morning in a panic
even though you're totally safe

or

never have the reflexes to truly
understand when you're in a
really bad situation?

Would you rather
never be able to keep a secret
or
never be able to lie?

Would you rather
give up going to concerts
or
going to the movies?

Would you rather

wake up every morning with
no teeth, but your teeth grow
back throughout the day

or

have your teeth retreat into your
gums throughout the day as if you're
Benjamin Button–ing at warp speed?

Would you rather

be 24 for the rest of your life

or

42 for the rest of your life?

CHOOSE YOUR OWN SHAME

Behold, a horror buffet of life's worst-case scenarios. There are no happy endings here, just you choosing the lesser of two ridiculous evils. Which brand of embarrassment or social exile can you live with? Which surprise bodily fluid would ruin a night out the least? Choose the best, but prepare for the worst.

Would you rather
let your partner dress you
or
style your hair for one week?

Would you rather
confess your darkest secrets to a
theater full of your work friends
or
have a theater full of your work
friends form a line to confess their
darkest secrets to you?

Would you rather
have the intimate details of
your relationship broadcast
over social media
or
turned into a Broadway show?

Would you rather
everyone knew whenever you farted
or
whenever you had a dirty thought?

Would you rather
everyone knew you'd
just clogged a toilet
or
knew you used to eat
glue as a kid?

Would you rather
trip over nothing and scrape up
your face in front of a large crowd
or
smile widely at a large crowd
of people with your teeth visibly
full of broccoli?

Would you rather
spend an entire day with
your butt hanging out
or
with your internet search
history on display?

Would you rather
be forced to tell everyone around
you what you really thought of
them for 24 hours
or
hear what they really thought
of you for 24 hours?

Would you rather
have diarrhea while waiting
in a long line
or
while riding on a short
roller-coaster?

Would you rather
vomit on a plane full of people,
but you can't smell it,
or
be on a plane in which someone
else vomits, but you *can* smell it?

Would you rather
your partner wear a
Richard Nixon mask
or
a Bill Clinton mask during sex?

Would you rather
get caught stealing
or
lying?

Would you rather
ugly-cry in front of a huge
crowd of strangers
or
pee your pants in front of them?

Would you rather
get caught picking your nose
or
looking at the tissue after you
blew your nose?

Would you rather
always have smelly feet
or
smelly armpits?

Would you rather
have hands covered in scabs
or
have constantly peeling lips?

Would you rather
be a horrible person who never
picks up after their dog
or
a jerk who throws trash
out the car window?

Would you rather
find a hard drive with the
only copy of your sworn
enemy's darkest secrets
or
the only copy of your
own darkest secrets?

Would you rather
always have clammy hands
or
clammy feet?

Would you rather
have to relive your most
embarrassing moment
or
witness your partner's most
embarrassing moment?

Would you rather
accidentally call your boss "Mom"
or
call them the name you use for
them behind their back?

Would you rather
be responsible for giving
your partner a bad haircut
or
a bad fake tan?

Would you rather
get caught peeing in a pool
or
cheating on a test?

Would you rather
walk into a meeting with toilet paper
on your shoe
or
pit stains on your shirt?

Would you rather
accidentally send a dirty text
to your boss
or
to your cousin?

Would you rather
everyone know you invested all
your money in Pokémon cards
but sold them right before they
got really valuable
or
that you keep all your Beanie Babies
in a climate-controlled glass safe
and say good night to them
every evening?

Would you rather
find out you're dating
a former cult leader
or
a former cult follower?

Would you rather
everyone know when
you're embarrassed
or
when you're scared?

Would you rather

be seen waiting in front of a regular
door thinking it's automatic
or
be seen trying to pull a door clearly
marked "Push"?

Would you rather

take a sip of wine and
miss your mouth
or
drop a saucy meatball in your
lap during a fancy dinner?

Would you rather
realize halfway through the day that
you've put on two different shoes
or
that you've been wearing your
shirt backward?

Would you rather
loudly fart while saying
your wedding vows
or
while giving a presentation
to your whole company?

Would you rather
call someone by the wrong
name to their face
or
wave at someone enthusiastically
only to realize it's not the person you
thought it was?

Would you rather
get the response
"We've met before"
or
the response "No, it's not. I heard
you suck!" when you say "Nice to
meet you!" to someone?

Would you rather
find out your partner has kept
every bandage
or
every Q-Tip they've ever used?

Would you rather
have to go to the hospital because
you ate a decorative ear of corn
thinking it was real
or
because you got a golf ball
stuck in your butt?

LIVE THAT FANTASY

You can live the dream, but you can't live *all* the dreams. Even when you're thinking big, you must choose which doors to throw open and which paths must be forever left untaken. Will you choose brains or beauty? Vast, unimaginable wealth or the respect and love of others? Ask these questions to find out what you truly desire.

Would you rather
pair up with your significant other
to fight zombies
or
vampires?

Would you rather
be rich but have no street smarts
(e.g., you're constantly sending
money to Nigerian princes)
or
be poor but savvy?

Would you rather
spend the rest of your life
living on a beach
or
living in the mountains?

Would you rather
never have to work again but
be bored every day
or
work every day at a job you love and
be really busy all the time?

Would you rather
be known for being smart
or
for being kind?

Would you rather
have a talking pet that only you can
understand, and everyone thinks
you've lost your mind,
or
a talking pet that everyone can
understand, but it has no filter
and talks about the horrible
things you do?

Would you rather
speak any language
or
play any musical instrument?

Would you rather
eat whatever you wanted and
never gain weight
or
drink as much alcohol as you
wanted and never get a hangover?

Would you rather
be famous and broke
or
rich and unknown?

Would you rather
look young forever
or
feel young forever?

Would you rather
live a dangerous and exciting life
or
a safe and boring one?

Would you rather
be a great artist with a tortured soul
or
have no artistic talent but be
blissfully happy?

Would you rather
live in a super-cute tiny house that's
too small to have friends over
or
an old mansion that's full of
friendly ghosts?

Would you rather
work 60 hours a week and
earn six figures
or
work regular hours and earn
half as much?

Would you rather

travel by private jet (even short distances) but feel guilty about your contribution to climate change

or

travel only by Rollerblades that make it impossible for you to go far away?

Would you rather

own the oldest archeological artifact

or

the biggest jewel?

Would you rather
be the CEO at a failing company
or
an entry-level worker at a
successful one?

Would you rather
take only one vacation every five
years but afford to do whatever
you wanted
or
take a budget vacation every year?

Would you rather

become rich and famous for co-creating a trashy reality TV show with your partner

or

for co-authoring a how-to book about sex positions?

Would you rather

have the fastest technology but need to charge it every hour

or

slow technology but need to charge it only once a week?

Would you rather
stay at the nicest hotel in the world
or
eat at the finest restaurant
in the world?

Would you rather
own a luxurious yacht
or
a private plane?

Would you rather
have a personal chef
or
a personal driver?

Would you rather
have one day to do whatever you
wanted without getting hurt
or
one day to say whatever you
wanted without anyone's feelings
getting hurt?

Would you rather
discover a new flavor
or
a new color?

Would you rather
go on a couple's vacation
to Jurassic Park
or
Westworld?

Would you rather
wake up every morning and look
great in the first outfit you put on
or
wake up every morning with
perfect hair?

Would you rather
win a gold medal in solo
synchronized swimming
or
poodle clipping?

Would you rather
be able to control the weather
or
the traffic?

Would you rather
have your dream body
or
your dream face?

Would you rather
live in a place you loved but that
everyone else hated
or
a place you hated but that
everyone else loved?

Would you rather
spend a year broke but able to
travel wherever you wanted
or
have $100,000 to spend in a year
but be unable to leave your home?

Would you rather
get away with one huge crime
or
get to make one new law?

Would you rather
rule over the entire world
or
live as a simple citizen in a utopia?

Would you rather
be remembered for doing one
bad thing
or
not remembered even though you
did a lot of good things?

Would you rather
visit a place you've always
wanted to go
or
learn a skill you've always
wanted to learn?

ALL ABOUT THE XOXO

Relationships are fascinating, with all sorts of twists and turns. May we present the opportunity to discuss decisions you never thought you'd have to make before they happen? From the silly to the sexy, here are some questions to raise your eyebrows . . . or singe them off.

Would you rather
role-play as Homer and Marge
from *The Simpsons*
or
Morticia and Gomez from
The Addams Family?

Would you rather
give up holding hands
or
or spooning?

Would you rather
go out on a date dressed in
medieval costumes
or
dressed as Furries?

Would you rather
have sex on an uncomfortable
waterbed
or
a mysteriously stained futon?

Would you rather
your partner make extremely
loud sounds
or
absolutely no sound at all
while making love?

Would you rather
invite Beyoncé
or
Jay-Z to join your throuple?

Would you rather
your partner pick you up for
a date on a unicycle
or
a Segway?

Would you rather
give up morning sex
or
afternoon delights?

Would you rather
you and your partner have
matching nipple piercings
or
neck tattoos?

Would you rather
find out your partner used to be a
model for romance novel covers
or
a competitor on a
reality dating show?

Would you rather
walk in on your parents having sex
or
have your parents walk in
on you having sex?

Would you rather
make out while listening to
the *Moby-Dick* audiobook
or
a recording of cats in heat?

Would you rather
take a vow of celibacy
or
a vow of silence for a month?

Would you rather
be wooed with gifts
or
compliments?

Would you rather
always have to share half
your food on dates
or
never get to taste your partner's
order no matter what?

Would you rather
write someone an embarrassingly
bad poem confessing your love
or
make them a playlist of all
Kidz Bop songs?

Would you rather
explore foreplay with
a new bedroom toy
or
a new bedroom costume?

Would you rather
receive an erotic massage
from your partner
or
watch an erotic movie with them?

Would you rather
be known as the sexiest
or
the most romantic
significant other?

Would you rather
try bondage
or
attempt to join the
Mile High Club?

Would you rather
be with someone who thinks
you're funny and dumb
or
smart but not funny?

Would you rather
receive a steamy sext from
your partner
or
wake up to find they've vacuumed
the house, done the dishes, and
finished the laundry?

Would you rather
have phone sex
or
exchange dirty pictures?

Would you rather
have a threesome with your boss
or
a stranger chosen at random?

Would you rather
switch bodies with your partner
for one night
or
sleep with an exact copy of yourself?

Would you rather
always be on top
or
always be on bottom?

Would you rather
have sex after binge-watching
all the *Saw* movies
or
after eating a gallon of spaghetti?

Would you rather
go on a date to a murder
mystery weekend
or
shopping for antiques?

Would you rather
reenact the pottery scene
from *Ghost*
or
the rain scene from *The Notebook*?

Would you rather
star in a porn movie
or
stumble across a porn movie
your partner is in?

Would you rather
have a low-key wedding and go
on a luxurious honeymoon
or
have a super-fancy wedding and
go easy on the honeymoon?

Would you rather
fake an orgasm
or
find out your partner faked one?

Would you rather
have 3 people at your wedding
or
300?

Would you rather
sit on the same side of a
restaurant booth
or
across from each other on
a date with your partner?

Would you rather
cook dinner for your date but hot dogs must be the main ingredient
or
serenade your date using nothing but remixes of "Tubthumping" by Chumbawumba?

Would you rather
get caught talking to your partner in a baby voice
or
feeding each other in front of your coworkers?

POP CULTURE HOT TAKES

Celebs. They're just like us! And like us, they must also make and be involved in ridiculous choices. Will you get "the Rachel" or "the Ross"? Which Real Housewife would you let dog-sit for you? Could you survive a cross-country road trip with the boys of BTS? Warning: Your personal hot takes *will* be revealed. Answer these questions wisely.

Would you rather
have to watch the entire series of
Fifty Shades of Grey
or
Twilight every day?

Would you rather
go out for one night with the
characters of *Sex and the City*
or
Succession?

Would you rather
have Stephen King
or
Danielle Steel write
your biography?

Would you rather
spend a day with John Lennon
or
Elvis Presley before they
were famous?

Would you rather
be best friends with Hulk from
The Avengers
or
Beast from *X-Men*?

Would you rather
have been at Studio 54 in its heyday
or
at Woodstock?

Would you rather
be forced to watch *Hamilton*, even
though you hate musicals,
or
The Ring, even though you hate
scary movies?

Would you rather
compete with your partner on
The Amazing Race
or
against your partner on
The Great British Baking Show?

Would you rather
hang out with Johnny Depp's
character from *Pirates of
the Caribbean*
or
his character from *Charlie and
the Chocolate Factory*?

Would you rather
live with the Na'vi people in *Avatar*
or
the people of Wakanda in
Black Panther?

Would you rather
ride in the DeLorean from
Back to the Future
or
the *Millennium Falcon* from
Star Wars?

Would you rather
have been seen backstage in
2000 with *NSYNC
or
Eminem?

Would you rather
lose on *Top Chef*
or
win the annual Nathan's
Hot Dog Eating Contest?

Would you rather
go to a job interview wearing
Lady Gaga's meat dress
or
Björk's swan dress?

Would you rather
be an overnight viral YouTube star
or
a beloved author whose work isn't
appreciated until after your death?

Would you rather
be famous for having the world's
largest collection of troll dolls
or
Pogs?

Would you rather
cook dinner for your partner
or
have your partner do the cooking
and the meal is publicly judged
by Gordon Ramsay?

Would you rather
have been a guest at Victoria and
David Beckham's wedding
or
a guest at a dinner party with the
Spice Girls?

Would you rather
go on a quest to destroy the "One Ring" from *The Lord of the Rings*
or
fight in the games in
The Hunger Games?

Would you rather
win a special couples' edition
of *Jeopardy!*
or
Wheel of Fortune?

Would you rather
spend Christmas with the Grinch
or
with Jack Skellington from *The Nightmare Before Christmas*?

Would you rather
be infamous for a sex tape
that everyone remembers, like
Kim Kardashian,
or
for being sentenced to a short prison
stint that everybody forgets about,
like Martha Stewart?

Would you rather
take a cross-country road trip with
all the boys from BTS and have
a lot of silly fun
or
spend two weeks in a log cabin
with Stevie Nicks and be changed
by her hard-won wisdom?

Would you rather
have been a member of the Rat Pack
or
the Brat Pack?

Would you rather
have partied at the Factory
with Andy Warhol
or
at the Viper Room with
Courtney Love?

Would you rather
have EGOT status
or
win a Nobel Prize?

Would you rather

have been in the audience at the VMAs when Kanye West interrupted Taylor Swift onstage

or

at the Oscars when *La La Land* mistakenly "won" Best Picture over *Moonlight*?

Would you rather

be friends with Prince William and Kate Middleton

or

Prince Harry and Meghan Markle?

Would you rather
be a member of the *Simpsons* family
or
the *Sopranos* family?

Would you rather
be known as an expert at doing
the moonwalk
or
the running man?

Would you rather
spend a day in the life of Oprah
or
Rihanna?

Would you rather
be infamous for lip-syncing
at your live performances
or
having a body double dance for
you in your music videos?

Would you rather
get the Beatles' bowl cut
or
"the Rachel" haircut?

Would you rather
have Crystal Pepsi
or
"Supersize" meals at McDonald's
make a permanent comeback?

Would you rather
be a patient at the hospital from
Grey's Anatomy
or
House?

Would you rather
have a rap battle with Snoop Dogg
or
a dance-off with Britney Spears?

BACK TO THE FUTURE

The future, the past, the entire human time line is open for business. Whom would you save? Where and when would you live? How would you change the past? How would you choose to affect our future? These extremely difficult choices will force you to finally admit what you would sacrifice to ride a dinosaur.

Would you rather
travel back in time with your
partner to save a historical
leader from assassination
or
assassinate one of history's
greatest villains?

Would you rather
the internet had never
been invented
or
that cell phones had never
been invented?

Would you rather
travel back in time 100 years and
have the option to come back
or
forward in time 100 years and
have to stay there forever?

Would you rather
time-travel with no choice in
where you went
or
travel back to a specific day, but it is
the worst day of your life?

Would you rather
see cancer cured
or
climate change reversed in
your lifetime?

Would you rather
go back in time and witness the
invention of the printing press
or
the invention of the automobile?

Would you rather
live without electricity
or
without the telephone?

Would you rather
live in a future where the population
was surveilled all the time, knowing
that it could prevent and
solve all crime,
or
where you were never surveilled
but where crime is completely
out of control?

Would you rather
live in a future where everyone used
yoga balls as chairs
or
where everyone walked around in
those shoes with individual toes?

Would you rather
save one currently endangered
species from extinction
or
bring back one extinct species and
give them another shot?

Would you rather

stop the *Titanic* from sinking
(saving lives but denying us James
Cameron's *Titanic*)
or
save the *Hindenburg* from crashing
(unglamorous, but it could mean the
adoption of travel by blimp)?

Would you rather

travel to the past and get rich
and famous by using your
modern technology
or
be given future technology
in the present?

Would you rather
visit the past but be unable
to change it
or
know the future, but no one
believes you?

Would you rather
visit past you
or
get a visit from your future self?

Would you rather

be rich and powerful 1,000 years ago
or
be rich and powerful 1,000 years in
the future, even though you have no
idea what that means?

Would you rather

travel back in time and fall in love
with someone who turned out to
be your ancestor
or
find out your current partner was
your descendant who traveled back
in time from the future?

Would you rather
be able to redo the last five minutes
whenever you wanted
or
redo a whole day but only
once a month?

Would you rather
that all technological progress
stopped but the world lived in peace
or
that technology improved at an even
faster rate but war still existed?

Would you rather
be the first person in history
to test out a flying car
or
a personal jetpack?

Would you rather
attend the premiere of a
Shakespeare play
or
watch Leonardo da Vinci finish
the *Mona Lisa*?

Would you rather
be trapped in a *Groundhog Day*–esque time loop, living the same day repeatedly,
or
not be able to remember anything that happened more than 10 years ago?

Would you rather
travel to the past and discover which famous historical miracles and myths *actually* happened
or
travel to the future and find out if we ever colonize space?

Would you rather
know what the future held for
everyone but yourself
or
know your own future but no
one else's?

Would you rather
give up your life on Earth to become
the first person to live on Mars
or
have to stay on Earth while everyone
else got the option to live in space?

Would you rather
swap bodies
or
swap minds with your partner
for one day?

Would you rather
get a chip implanted in your head
so you can search your brain for
information like the internet
or
be able to use your mouth like a
human Bluetooth speaker to play
any song you wanted?

Would you rather
live in a world without the internet
or
without the polio vaccine?

Would you rather
have to go back to using a Walkman
or
your first pair of headphones?

Would you rather

go back in time to ride a dinosaur knowing that this action would prevent the invention of democracy

or

visit the future to discover that you're considered one of the worst figures in history?

Would you rather

humans evolved to have night vision

or

unbreakable skin?

Would you rather
that future travel options included
fun hoverboards
or
instant teleporters?

Would you rather
clone the pet you had as a child
or
clone yourself so there's a backup
if you ever need one?

Would you rather
have the technology to create an
infinite number of replicas of one
person, but it can't be you,
or
just one replica of one person,
and it can only be you?

Would you rather
modify your body with animal parts
and abilities limited to what already
exists in nature
or
with bionic robot parts that can do
anything, but you lose your emotions
the more you change?

Would you rather
spend your whole life preparing for
an apocalypse that never comes
or
get caught up in a huge disaster
with no preparation?

Would you rather
be celebrated right now for
an invention that makes only
a few lives better
or
celebrated for an invention that
makes thousands of lives better long
after you're dead?

THE JUST PLAIN WEIRD

Welcome to Bonkersville. Population: two. Why limit yourself to realism when you can play in the fields of pure imagination? Sci-fi, magic, abstract moral quandaries, and deep, deep weirdness— sometimes, the silliest questions can reveal the most profound truths.

Would you rather
find yourself and your partner
in the Upside Down
(from *Stranger Things*)
or
the Land of Oz?

Would you rather
fight Bigfoot
or
a lake monster?

Would you rather
be hunted by a deer
or
ridden by a horse?

Would you rather
have fully cooked chicken wings
instead of arms
or
fully cooked chicken drumsticks
instead of legs?

Would you rather
have sex with Medusa (yes, the snakes are absolutely involved)
or
sex with a Siren on a rocky outcropping by the ocean (and yes, sailors *will* gawk at you)?

Would you rather
get to choose your height when you wake up every morning
or
your weight?

Would you rather
be able to communicate with
dead humans
or
with living animals?

Would you rather
have telekinesis
or
telepathy?

Would you rather
find out if aliens
or
ghosts were real?

Would you rather
accidentally summon Bloody Mary
or
find yourself face-to-face
with Pennywise?

Would you rather
confirm the existence of mermaids
but find out that they're total jerks
or
find out that whales are a hoax?

Would you rather
have a pet leopard
or
a pet eagle?

Would you rather
have to box with a
human-size cockroach
or
a human-size snake?

Would you rather
have infinite life as a vampire,
having to murder people by
drinking their blood,
or
as an android whose technology
will someday be outdated
and irreparable?

Would you rather
go to school at Hogwarts
or
Harvard?

Would you rather
that everyone *thought* you got
abducted by aliens, even though it
never happened,
or
that you *actually* got abducted by
aliens, but no one believed you?

Would you rather
defend yourself against a werewolf
with a teeny-tiny fork
or
an oversize inflatable baseball bat?

Would you rather
have a flying carpet
or
a flying umbrella as your main
mode of transportation?

Would you rather
uncover the truth about Area 51
or
the Bermuda Triangle?

Would you rather
confirm the existence of unicorns
but not have any proof
or
have proof that no one believes?

Would you rather
be able to cast spells, but only one
per day,
or
be super strong all the time?

Would you rather
take shelter in the countryside
or
in the city in the case of an alien
invasion?

Would you rather
have super-strong sight
or
super-strong hearing?

Would you rather
own a shark (and assume all the
responsibilities)
or
be forced to work for someone who
owns multiple sharks?

Would you rather
hurt no one but always feel
hurt yourself
or
hurt everyone but always feel
just fine?

Would you rather
be covered in fried chicken skin and
be able to remove it, even though
it's painful to get off,
or
have to leave the fried chicken
skin on and deal with it?

Would you rather
live in an enchanted forest with
wizards and centaurs
or
in a space station with aliens and
sentient robots?

Would you rather
own magic shoes that make you run
really fast but squeak terribly
or
a magic hat that can conjure
anything when you wear it but gives
you really bad hat hair?

Would you rather
be marooned on an island with
someone who's obsessed with
Civil War reenactments
or
adult train sets?

Would you rather
that dolphins
or
pandas got the right to vote?

Would you rather
be able to camouflage yourself in
any environment
or
climb anything like a spider so you
could hide anywhere you wanted?

Would you rather
be able to see the dreams of others
or
record and play back your own?

Would you rather

live in a world with multiple smaller gods that come down to earth and act just like people (flirting, arguing, causing drama)

or

in a world with one god who never speaks to anybody and who you can't be sure is doing anything useful?

Would you rather

be haunted by a ghost for your whole life

or

possessed by demon for a short time?

Would you rather
have the power to bring the
dead back to life
or
travel back in time?

Would you rather
come back to life as a ghost
or
a zombie?

About the Authors

Sanji Moore is a Brooklyn-based writer, the creator of As You 'Wich (a game about sandwiches), and a certified human resources professional. She enjoys traveling, knitting and crocheting, cooking and baking, and playing pranks on her husband. When she's not being a little devil, she plays games on her phone and watches period dramas on TV with her best friend and dog, Pepper.

Taylor Moore is the founder of Fortunate Horse, the studio behind the award-winning podcasts *Rude Tales of Magic, Fun City*, and *Oh These, Those Stars of Space!*; truTV's *Sex Your Food* series; and *Fortunate Horse Magazine*, a magazine for and about fortunate horses. You can follow (or yell at) him online at @taylordotbiz. Any comments or criticisms regarding the questions in this book can be directed to his assistant, Pepper.

Hi there,

We hope you enjoyed reading *Would You Rather? Questions for Couples*. If you have any questions or concerns about your book, or have received a damaged copy, please contact customerservice@penguinrandomhouse.com. We're here and happy to help.

Also, please consider writing a review on your favorite retailer's website to let others know what you thought of the book!

Sincerely,
The Zeitgeist Team